Alexander Hamilton's
New York City

D1290962

Dona Herweck Rice

Consultant

Vanessa Ann Gunther, Ph.D.
Chapman University

Publishing Credits

Rachelle Cracchiolo, M.S.Ed., *Publisher*
Conni Medina, M.A.Ed., *Managing Editor*
Emily R. Smith, M.A.Ed., *Content Director*
Seth Rogers, *Editor*
Robin Erickson, *Senior Graphic Designer*

Image credits: Cover and pp. 1, 4, 21 (top) North Wind Picture Archives;
Read and Respond page, pp. 8, 10, 12–13, 16, 19, 20, 27, 32, back page New
York Public Library Digital Collections; pp. 2–3, 14, 18, 24 Granger, NYC; p. 5
Photo Researchers, Inc/Alamy Stock Photo; p. 7 Courtesy of Geographicus
Rare Antique Maps; p. 11 (top) Len Holsborg/Alamy Stock Photo, (bottom)
Album/Prisma/Newscom; p. 12 Current source: sewerhistory.org. Original
source: Philadelphia Suburban Water Co.; p. 15 Library of Congress Prints
& Photographs Division [LC-USZ62-55675]; p. 17 Carl Otto von Kienbusch,
Jr. Memorial Collection, Princeton University Art Museum; p. 22 Library of
Congress Prints & Photographs Division [LC-USZ62-70508]; p. 22 New York
Stock Exchange Archives; p. 25 Beyond My Ken/License: Creative Commons
BY-SA 4.0/https://goo.gl/6gbpbO; p. 28 Theo Wargo/Getty Images; p. 29
United States Treasury Bureau of Engraving and Printing; all other images from
iStock and/or Shutterstock

Teacher Created Materials
5301 Oceanus Drive
Huntington Beach, CA 92649-1030
http://www.tcmpub.com
ISBN 978-1-4258-6351-7
© 2017 Teacher Created Materials, Inc.

Table of Contents

Greatest City in the World

It is alive and **frenetic**, varied and diverse. It is bound by water but reaches for the sky. It is New York City, the sparkling gem on the shores of the Atlantic. Some people say it is the greatest city in the world.

But this is not today's New York. It is the New York of long ago—a New York that you can still experience if you know where to find it. The framework of the modern city was etched into this long-ago metropolis. Yet, while much of the old city has crumbled away, if you close your eyes and imagine, you can bring it to life. You can hear the gulls cry at the wide and bustling bayside **port** where trade flourishes on passing ships. You can hear the clomping of horseshoes and the rattling of wooden carts rolling along the narrow, paved roads that wind through the growing city. You can feel the shade of countless trees that line the byways as you walk past the tall wood and stone houses. And you can smell the ocean breeze that wafts down one of the few wide roads in the city, aptly known as Broad Way.

It is the New York of a developing nation. And it is the New York of Alexander Hamilton—the Founding Father who made it his home.

Alexander Hamilton, around age 15

upper Manhattan Island in the late 1700s

Alexander Hamilton

Hamilton was born in the West Indies. He came to America in his teens to make his way in the world. His passion for knowledge, growth, and making a name for himself not only shaped the man he would become but also a new nation—the United States of America.

Population Explosion

When Hamilton first came to New York City, it was the second largest city in the colonies. There were about 20,000 residents. Today, its expanding borders and dense population make it the largest city in the United States. This city has more than 8.5 million people.

Around Town

Little remains of New York as it was in 1664. That's the year that marks the official birth of the city. Some of the original street names are still there. The winding layout of streets in lower Manhattan remains as it was in those days, in contrast to the grid of roadways that crisscrosses the more modern sections of the city.

Alexander Hamilton arrived in New York in 1772. By then, the city had blossomed into one of the largest cities in the colonies. Together with Boston and Philadelphia, it was **primed** to shape the foundation of a new nation. Commerce thrived, politics pulsed, and cultures merged around every corner.

Homes and businesses filled the expanse of New York from the Battery to the Common, now called City Hall Park. At the lower end of Manhattan, you will find the Battery. It was given its name in colonial days. It was there that the Dutch set up **batteries** to protect their trading post. The name stuck even though the guns and the trading post are long gone. The Battery is also of note for one more essential reason. For hundreds of years, it was the entry point to New York for millions of immigrants. It is, in fact, where Hamilton first stepped onto the banks of his new homeland.

New York City has always been home to both incredibly wealthy individuals as well as people living in the depths of poverty. Wall Street and Hanover Square near Pearl and Stone Streets were **tony** sections. The poor crowded into shabby dwellings or lived on the streets. Crime flourished, particularly in poor neighborhoods. Bridewell Prison was built to deal with this growing problem.

New Amsterdam

First known as New Amsterdam and settled by colonists from the Netherlands, Great Britain took possession of the area and renamed it New York in 1664. Though the British took control, they worked hard to include the Dutch colonists and their customs as the city grew. Dutch influence is still present.

Broadway Today

Hamilton has become a modern-day celebrity. This is all due to the Broadway smash hit *Hamilton: An American Musical*. The play and music were written by the show's original star, Lin-Manuel Miranda.

MAP
of
NEW YORK I.
with the adjacent Rocks
and other remarkable
Parts of
HELL-GATE.
By Thoˢ Kitchin Senʳ
Hydrographer to his
Majesty.

b.b. Barracks built for American Winter
Quarters, and burnt when the Kings
Troops landed at Fregs Point.

Green Spaces

New Yorkers walked around town for business and pleasure. Many people enjoyed the gardens in Hanover Square. Hamilton himself might have walked there, although he was most often spotted walking along the banks of the Hudson River. As a student, he also paced Batteau Street—now Dey Street—thinking and studying.

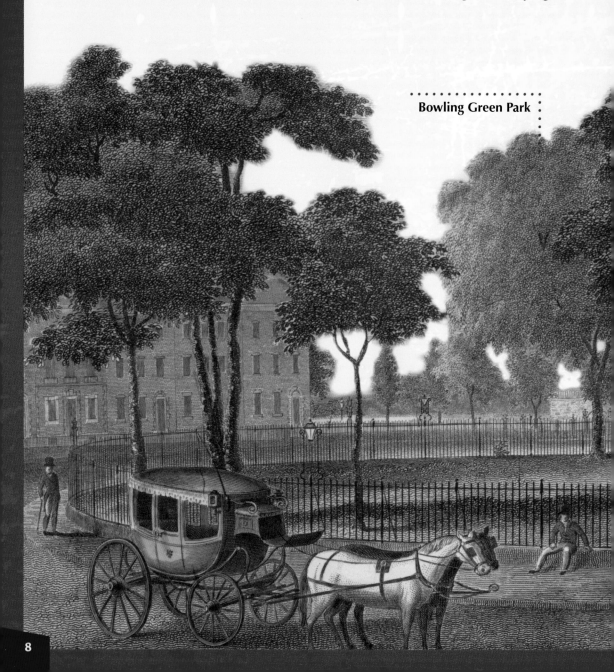

Bowling Green Park

In 1733, Bowling Green Park was established "for the Recreation and Delight of the inhabitants of the city." It was the first official park of New York. The city paid rent to three men for the use of Bowling Green Park and for maintaining it. The rent was one **peppercorn** per year.

Typical New Yorkers

John Adams, the second president of the United States, said of New Yorkers, "They talk very loud, very fast, and all together." People might think he was talking about New Yorkers today. They also have the reputation for fast-paced talk and activity.

Gardens

Many different garden styles could be found in colonial New York City, including landscape gardens and formal gardens. Landscape gardens are made to look natural, with lush overgrowth and small ponds. Formal gardens have well-maintained and trimmed plants, often with elaborate fountains. Both types of garden can be found in the city today.

Paving the Way

Many streets were named after their defining characteristics. For example, Canal Street followed the path of a stream. Stone Street, which had previously been known as Duke Street, got its new name because it was one of the first to be paved with cobblestones.

Merchants

Merchants Coffee House was the scene of many significant historic events. This includes a public meeting after the Battles of Lexington and Concord at the start of the Revolutionary War. It was a place of public importance until 1804 when it burned down.

Getting Around

Traveling around town was fairly easy, as most of the streets were paved. People walked or rode horses, and **draymen** pulled horse-drawn carts. Those who could afford carriages used them.

But even with pavement, the streets were dirty, and, of course, walking took effort. The rich bypassed these annoyances, but most people just had to learn to live with them.

King's Arms Tavern

Dining Out

New York has long been **renowned** for its restaurants. Of special note in Hamilton's time were coffee houses, such as the first King's Arms. In such places, a customer could sit in a private, curtained booth to enjoy coffee. In the upper rooms, assemblies of various kinds—including trials—were held. Mail was often picked up from and delivered to coffee houses as well.

Taverns also abounded through the city. At the corner of Pearl and Broad Streets sat the Fraunces Tavern. Built as a home in 1719, a West Indian man bought the building in 1762 and converted it into a tavern. It was very popular. Before the Revolution, it was a frequent meeting place for Patriots. The building stands today.

Fraunces Tavern

Fire!

A few eighteenth century buildings survive today. However, many were destroyed over time in three great fires that swept through New York in 1776, 1835, and 1845. Massive rebuilding took place after each tragedy.

More About Water

Finding fresh, clean water in the city was a challenge. At one time, the Manhattan Water Company made a system of log water pipes to deliver water to those who could afford it. Of note is the company's founder, Aaron Burr—the man who would kill Hamilton in an 1804 duel.

Making a Home

In Hamilton's day, the houses in New York were built similarly to those that immigrants remembered from their home countries. Each was often constructed around a large central chimney to provide warmth to the whole structure. Timber-framed homes were two stories tall. They had steep and sloping roofs.

In time, stone and brick were used for building materials as well. Craftsmen built mansions and showplaces for the New York elite. One of the oldest surviving buildings in New York is the Governor's House, built in 1708. It was built on Governor's Island in Upper New York Bay. Originally, it served as the home of a British lord.

Hamilton Heights

In upper Manhattan, there is an area known today as Hamilton Heights. In Hamilton's day, this area was known as Harlem Heights. It was all green hillsides with open farmland. In 1802, Hamilton established his family home there. He called it The Grange after his **ancestral** home in Scotland. Though Hamilton died just two years later, his name would live on. Due in part to the recent interest in the Founding Father, Hamilton Heights is experiencing a revival as well.

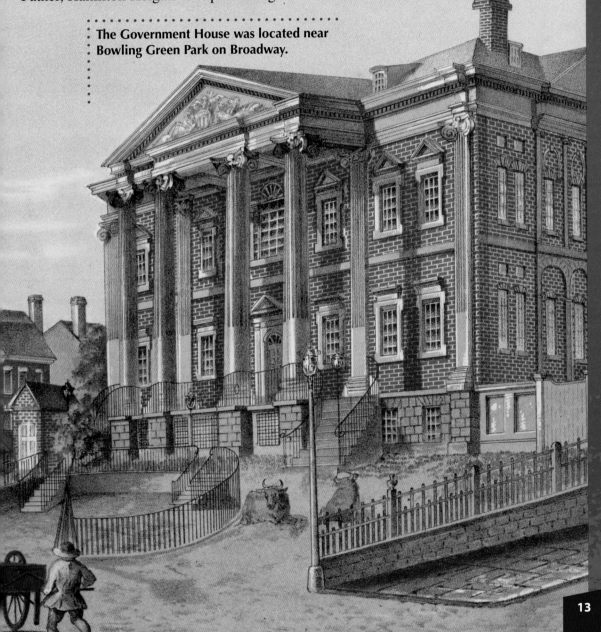

The Government House was located near Bowling Green Park on Broadway.

Cultural Hub

Since colonial times, New York has been known for **cultural diversity** and for bringing art and thought to life. When Hamilton arrived, there were already 14 languages spoken in the city. (There are about 800 spoken there today.) Many different religions were practiced. Some residents practiced no religion at all. Wealthy people enjoyed leisure, but the poor toiled most of their days. Everyone enjoyed dancing. Public halls were built for dances, and balls were held in the private homes of the wealthy. At such dances, the newly rich—those who were part of the growing merchant class—could easily be picked out from the longstanding wealthy. The latter group had trained all their lives with dance masters. The newly rich had not.

Theater is one of New York City's biggest cultural draws. The city had embraced this pastime long before Hamilton arrived. The first theater opened on Nassau Street in 1732. In 1750, two actors named Thomas Kean and Walter Murray opened a 280-seat theater. Then, the New Theatre on Chatham Street was opened in 1798. About 2,000 **patrons** of all classes could sit in this grand theater.

young George
Washington dancing
the minuet

Read All about It!

During the Revolution, the *New York Journal* printed insider information about the war. The British wanted to stop this, but they couldn't find the paper. The printer changed locations often to avoid capture.

Immigration

In Hamilton's day, thousands of immigrants flooded to New York City each year. Hamilton arrived from the West Indies. Most immigrants at the time, though, came from England, Scotland, and Ireland. The architects of the New Theatre were immigrants from France.

King's College

Education has long been an important part of New York life. Today's Columbia University got its start in 1754 as King's College. The campus was a political hotbed. Protests were often held there. People gathered near a tall pole at the center of the grounds. At the top of the pole was a weather vane in the shape of the word "Liberty."

Students at King's College took classes that focused on studies of the classics. The goal was to teach students how to reason, write, and speak persuasively. This way, they left the school as more cultured people. Hamilton was a student at King's College starting in 1774. However, he left his studies after just one year. He went to serve in the Revolutionary War. The college closed in 1776 because of the war.

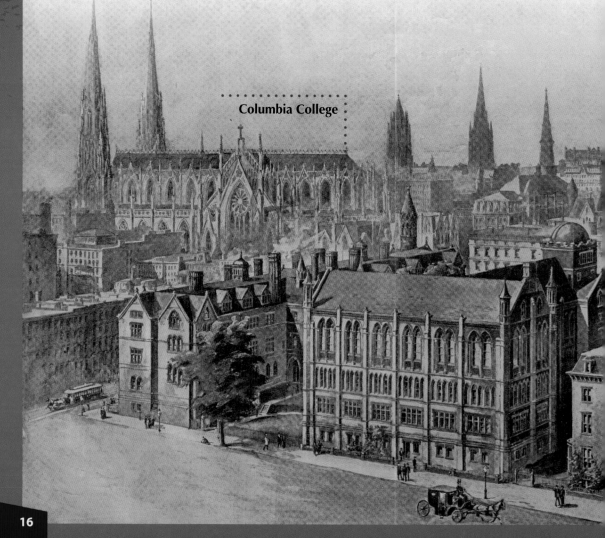

Columbia College

Hamilton worked with a number of people to reopen the college. Its name was changed to Columbia College in 1784. It became Columbia University in 1896. All students at the school were male. Women were not welcome as students until 1983.

undergraduate robes from the late 1700s

King of the North

King's College was located in the northern part of the city at the time, near the Hudson River. The college sat on land owned by Trinity Church, about one block from the Common (now City Hall Park).

College Dress

King's College students wore academic gowns and caps for their studies. These outfits were common for academics to wear at the time. Most colleges today only require students to wear these traditional clothes during graduation ceremonies.

More News

William Bradford set up the first printing press in New York in 1693. In 1725, he also established the first newspaper, the *New-York Gazette*. While the paper had a poor reputation, it paved the way for many other newspapers. New York's role as a news center began to take shape.

The Business of Slavery

In the early 1700s, about 40 percent of New York homes used slaves. New York City had the second highest percentage of slaves in the colonies. It was second only to Charleston, South Carolina. Slavery was undoubtedly a factor in New York's economic growth. After the Revolution, sentiments shifted. New York leaned strongly toward abolition.

Government and Finance

New York City was an early capital of the United States and home to the first secretary of the treasury. The city helped shape the new nation. During the war, it was as **relevant** as Boston and Philadelphia. After the war, it continued to play a key role in building the country.

In 1625, the Dutch built Fort Amsterdam at the southern tip of Manhattan. In 1683, it became the first meeting place for the New York legislature. It was demolished in 1790 to build a home for the nation's new president. But Washington never had the chance to live there. Before they finished, the capital was moved to Philadelphia for ten years. In 1800, it moved again to its final spot in Washington, D.C.

Though it is no longer the nation's capital, New York is thought of as the world's financial capital. Hamilton founded the Bank of New York in 1784. This bank set a standard for how all banks in the country would run. The New York **Stock** Exchange is also based in the city. It serves as a gauge for the **fiscal** health of the country.

Fort Amsterdam

U.S. Capital

New York's City Hall was constructed on Wall and Nassau Streets in early 1785. For about five years, the Congress of the Confederation made New York the nation's capital. City Hall was the first capitol building of the United States.

While City Hall was under construction, **delegates** met at Fraunces Tavern. When complete, the building was renamed Federal Hall. Congress met there for the first time in March 1789. Its first act was to count the votes in the national election. The new president, George Washington, took his oath of office there in April. A few months later, the Bill of Rights was introduced to Congress in Federal Hall.

The original building was destroyed in 1812. However, Washington's presence is still seen at the new Federal Hall. A statue honoring him is located in front of the hall, looking over Wall Street. Inside the hall, the Bible on which he was sworn in is on display.

Federal Hall

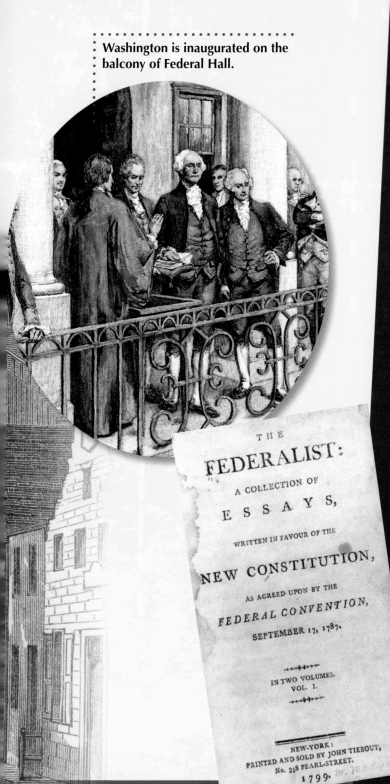

Washington is inaugurated on the balcony of Federal Hall.

One of Nine

New York City was one of eight national capitals before it permanently settled in Washington, D.C. One location—Lancaster, Pennsylvania—was only considered the capital for one day. Then, the capital had to move farther from the British Army.

The Federalist Papers

The United States Constitution was on a rocky path to state **ratification** when Alexander Hamilton stepped in. James Madison, John Jay, and he wrote a series of anonymous essays in favor of ratification. These essays became known as *The Federalist Papers.*

Roosevelts

The Bank of New York had many influential founders. One of the founders was Isaac Roosevelt. He was one of the first large-scale sugar refiners in New York City. Nearly 150 years later, his great grandson, Franklin Delano Roosevelt, would be elected as the 32nd president of the United States.

Under the Sycamore

A group of traders on Wall Street met under a sycamore tree outside their offices. These meetings led to the establishment of the New York Stock Exchange in 1792. They called their pact the Buttonwood Agreement. This was named after the buttonwood sycamore tree. A small sycamore still grows outside the exchange in tribute to the original traders.

Wall Street

In 1653, a tall wooden wall was built to the north of New Amsterdam to protect its residents against attacks from the north. The wall was taken down in 1699. But a street had already been shaped along the line of the wall. It was named—what else?—Wall Street.

In 1865, the first permanent New York Stock Exchange building was built. It was near the corner of Wall and Broad streets. Because it was there, Wall Street became known as a financial center. Only eight blocks long, Wall Street (and the surrounding area) are filled with today's most powerful financial institutions.

The Buttonwood Agreement

Bank of New York

In 1784, Hamilton and a small group of men established the Bank of New York. Hamilton wrote the bank's constitution. As secretary of the treasury, he also organized a loan to the federal government from the Bank of New York. That loan helped to establish credit for the country and develop its independence. The bank's stock was also the first stock traded on the New York Stock Exchange. Today, the bank stands at 1 Wall Street.

New York Stock Exchange

U.S. coins

Soul and Spirit

New York has always been home to a diverse group of faiths. Mainly focused on economic gain, people from many different backgrounds and religions settled in New York in its early days. Some of the settlers practiced no religion at all. This diversity is still present in New York.

In Hamilton's day, most New Yorkers belonged to churches. Many of them spent the bulk of their **Sabbaths** there. Hamilton was a Protestant and a deist, as many of his peers were. Deists believe in God but consider a moral life based in reason to be more important than anything else. Though he rarely attended services, Hamilton rented pews at Trinity Church. He even provided the church with free legal services when needed.

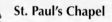

St. Paul's Chapel

New York was filled with many churches. Each one was home to a different religion. Religion was a personal matter, as it is today. People had the freedom to choose what they practiced without fear of harassment from the government. This freedom pleased many immigrants.

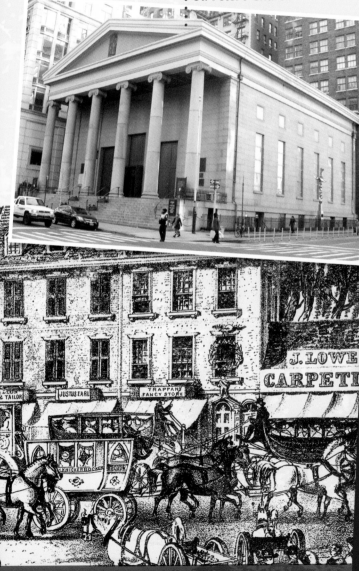

St. Peter's Church

Catholic Churches

Today, visitors to New York City are often enthralled by the architecture of the majestic Catholic cathedrals in the city. St. Peter's was the first Catholic church in New York. It was built in 1785 and reconstructed in 1836. The church stands at the corner of Barclay and Church Streets.

The Little Chapel that Stood

Built in 1764, St. Paul's Chapel is the oldest church in New York City. It's an Episcopalian church. George Washington and other Founding Fathers sometimes attended services there. Today, it is called "the little Chapel that stood." Despite its location across the street from the original World Trade Center, it was undamaged in the fall of the twin towers on September 11, 2001.

Reaching for the Sky

New York is known for tall skyscrapers that cast everything below in shadow. For 44 years, Trinity Church was actually the tallest building in New York. Its spire rose 280 feet (85 meters) above the ground. The New York World Building opened in 1890 and surpassed the church at 349 feet (106 meters).

Hamilton's Grave

Many historically important people are buried at Trinity Church Cemetery. Among them is Alexander Hamilton. His grave marker reads, in part, "The statesman of consummate wisdom, whose talents and virtues will be admired!" Due to the success of the Broadway show named after him, fans often visit this sacred spot.

Trinity Church

Church Street is a short street in lower Manhattan. It got its name from Trinity Church. Located near the New York Stock Exchange, at Wall Street and Broadway, Trinity Church was first built in 1698. It burned down during the Revolutionary War and was rebuilt in 1790. Then, a snowstorm badly damaged the building, and it was later torn down. The church structure that stands today was finished in 1846. It is known for its **Gothic** architecture. It was also one of the first churches in the United States to have stained glass windows. It stands proudly— but is now shadowed among the towering financial buildings that surround it.

Trinity Church, circa 1861

Trinity Church is also notable for a factor beyond its historical role and beauty. In 1705, the Queen of England gave the church a large section of land off Broadway. The church still owns a sizable portion of that land. There are now 26 buildings on it, housing millions of square feet of office space. Each rented space pays a sizable monthly rent to the church. The church makes millions of dollars in rent each year this way. It is, in fact, the richest parish in the world.

Trinity Church today

Hamilton's Manhattan

In *Hamilton: An American Musical*, the cast sings, "History is happening in Manhattan, and we just happen to be in the greatest city in the world!" It's a thought that many modern New Yorkers might share. It was always true for Hamilton. His New York City pulsed with activity and ideas. The growing city was propelled into the forefront of revolution and the foundation of a new nation.

Hamilton and the country boldly took steps onto a new shore. He helped lead the way to a world of possibility and promise for all. His hunger for **equity** and thirst for advancement helped spark a political revolution. They also ignited a revolution of ideas. The power of Hamilton's pen and strength of his will changed the course of a nation.

Hamilton's New York City was indeed a place where history was happening. In fact, he made it happen. "Look around, look around!" You can see it even to this day.

Lin-Manuel Miranda wrote and originally starred in *Hamilton: An American Musical.*

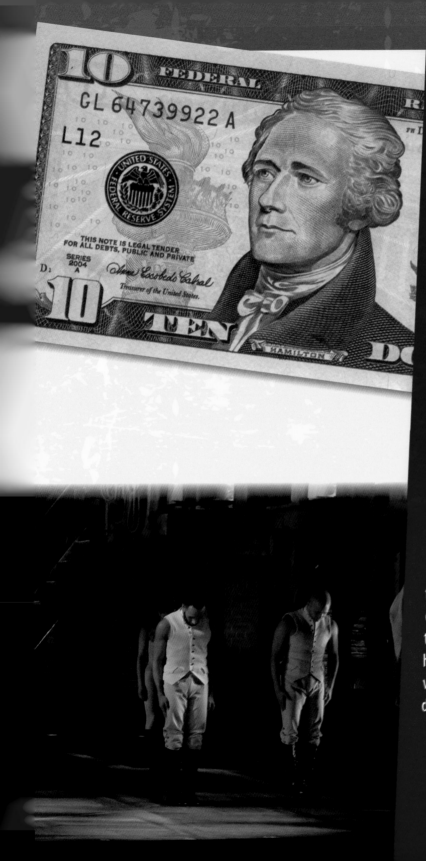

Saving Face

In 2015, it was announced that the picture on the United States $10 bill, which features Hamilton, would be changed. A public outcry followed, largely spurred by the popularity of *Hamilton*. In 2016, the plans to remove Hamilton from the bill were scrapped.

Why the Big Deal?

The show is critically acclaimed and has profoundly impacted the world beyond musical theater. It inspires people of all ages and walks of life to learn and explore U.S. history—and relate to it in ways they may never have done before.

Glossary

ancestral—related to a person's family who lived before him or her

batteries—military forts that house large guns and artillery for defense of an area

cultural diversity—variety of beliefs, habits, and traditions

delegates—people chosen by a group to represent the whole group's interests

draymen—people who drive horse-drawn carts used to deliver goods

equity—fairness

fiscal—financial; having to do with money

frenetic—fast and energetic

Gothic—related to a style of architecture that is noted for narrow, tall walls and tall, pointed arches, popular in twelfth to sixteenth century Europe

patrons—customers

peppercorn—a dried berry that is ground up to make pepper

port—place where ships are harbored, usually to load and unload goods; a town or city where this happens

primed—prepared; made ready

ratification—acceptance through votes

relevant—being directly related to a subject

renowned—well known and admired

Sabbaths—holy days, usually once a week, often Saturday or Sunday

stock—a share in the value of a company, which can be bought, sold, or traded

taverns—public houses where visitors can eat and drink

tony—expensive and highly fashionable

Index

Your Turn!

Above is a drawing of New York City from 1797. At the time, it was the largest city in the United States. Look closely at the image. Compare and contrast what you see to what you know about major cities today. How are things similar? How have things changed? Create an illustrated Venn diagram that compares cities today to what you see in this image of 1797 New York City.